The FIGHTING COLOURS of

Richard J. Caruana
50th Anniversary Collection

1: Saab 37 Viggen

History

Concept, artwork and overall design:
    © *Richard J. Caruana*

Printed version by:
MMPBooks.biz
ISBN: 978-83-66549-46-3

Acknowledgements:

Chris Syndham-Bailey
Steve Page
Mark Zerafa
Ola Born
Urban Lundqvist
André Nilsson
Andreas Klein
Tim Laming
Charles Stafrace

"We make aircraft". Three words that describe in a nutshell the Saab Aircraft Division and its long history as a leading designer and manufacturer of some of the most advanced aircraft in the world. In a brochure commemorating its first 50 years of activity (1937-1987) the company claims that it has "built up a knowledge base second to none. We design and develop. We test and produce. We follow up and support. In fact, we pride ourselves on a level of technology comparable with the best in world aviation".

Before proceeding to describe Saab's most important aircraft that was to serve from the '70s well into the 21st Century, it is fitting to take a brief look at the history of this extraordinary European company. Which though small compared to other major aircraft manufacturers, can claim to be one of the most technologically advanced in the world. Most of as aircraft are classics.

The original Svenska Aeroplan AB (Saab) was founded at Tröhattan in 1937 for the production of military aircraft. In 1939 this company was amalgamated with the Aircraft Division (ASJA) of the Svenska Järnvägsverkstäderna rolling stock factory at Linköping, where Saab

Saab AJ 37 Viggen 6-44 of F 6 seen in company with A32 6-23 Lansen at the time of the latter's retirement from front line service
(SAAB-Scania)

moved its head office and engineering departments. In 1950 Saab acquired a factory at Jonköping for the development and manutacture of airborne equipment. Other, post-war expansion included a bomb proof underground factory at Linköping and new production and engineering facilfties inLinköpin, Jonköping, Trollhättan and Gothernburg. The company's name was changed to Saab Aktiebolag in May 1965. During 1968 a decision was taken to merge the company with Scania-Vabis, another large Swedish automotive concern, to strengthen the two companies' position in their related fields. In the same year also, Malmö Flygindustri (MFI) was acquired.

System 37

The Saab 37 Viggen multi-mission combat aircraft was to become the major component in the System 37 weapon system for the Swedish Air Force (SwAF). In brief, System 37 comprised the Viggen aircraft with powerplant, airborne equipment, armament, ammunition and photographic equipment, special ground servicing equipment including test equipment and also special training equipment including simulators. Particular attention was paid to the optimum adaptation of System 37 to the SwAF base organisation and air defence control stem (STRIL 60).

From the outset, the Saab 37 was designed as a basic platform which could be readily adapted to fulfil four primary role: attack, interception, reconnaissance and training, thus providing the SwAF with a completely integrated weapons system based on the concept pioneered in the USA. Each mission-optimised version was to have a secondary role, for example, the attack variant had a secondary interceptor capability. The specification was highly demanding for its time and one that obviously called for a highly sophisticated warplane. Design definition was completed in 1962 and a development contract signed in October of that same year. The project was assigned the name Viggen (Thunderbolt). Prolonged research led to adoption of a then unique canard configuration for the combat aircraft that was to form the airborne component of the weapon system. This configuration, combined with engine thrust reversing, automatic speed control in the approach, a head-up display (HUD) and a landing gear designed for no-flare, high-sink-rate (carrier-type) landings, was adopted to provide an excellent STOL performance so that the Viggen would be able to operate from short runways and sections of roadway about 1,640ft in length, greatly increasing flexibility of dispersed operations. This capability was frequently demonstrated at major international airshows in Europe where spectators remaining in awe at the Viggen's short take-offs and incredibly tight turns. Combined with an afterburning derivative of the Pratt & Whitney JT8D turbofan, the configuration permitted the Saab 37 to cruise economically and at the same time possessed an acceleration and climb performance required for interception duties.

The Viggen's pilot sits strapped to a zero-zero ejection seat in an air-conditioned, heated and pressurised cockpit, protected by a bird-proof windscreen. Much of the capability of the aircraft is the result of the advanced contemporary avionics, including a HUD linked via an air-data computer to a digital fire-control system, ECM and radar warning equipment for its own

protection, Doppler radar and radar altimeter for navigation and a tactical instrument landing system plus a blind-landing guidance system for landing in any kind of weather, an important consideration in view of the Scandinavian environment. The Viggen was designed for long alert periods. An auxiliary power unit on the ground provided electric power for its equipment and cool or hot air as necessary. During high readiness alerts the engine could be idled with fuel spent being continuously replaced via a special fuel line. The pilot could accelerate immediately after take-off had been ordered. Long combat air patrols was achieved thanks to the low fuel consumption of the engine at reduced speeds.

Maintenance and servicing on the Viggen was facilitated by suitable location of equipment and good accessibility through the many inspection doors that cover one quarter of the total surface of the aircraft. Most work could take place at comfortable heights and the equipment was been grouped in such a way that line-replaceable units have a weight suitable for easy handling. Electronic equipment was of plug-in design. Part replacement times varied from five minutes for a radio to four hours for the engine, which could be replaced in the open. Of the total maintenance work, 46 per cent related to the engine, 23 per cent to the electronics and 31 per cent to the basic aircraft. Unique for Sweden was the fact that turn-round between missions could be carried out by a team of five conscript personnel under the command of a chief mechanic. The aircraft could be made ready for its next mission in less than 10 minutes. This requirement resulted in stringent demands on maintainability and a high level of personnel training.

Saab SF 37 Viggen, 37957, 21-56 now resident of the Essy Expozice Letecka A Kosmonautika Vojenské Muzeum in Kebely, Czech Republic. The camera fairing above the nosewheel door appears only on this side. At the time of the type's retirement national and identity markings were in black and all other markings toned down as well as can be noted from the air intake 'danger' sign (???)

Cockpit interior of the AJ 37 Viggen

The first of seven Viggen prototypes flew for the first time on 8 February 1967, and by April 1969 all six single-seat prototypes were flying. A number of airframe parts were also completed for static testing. Development priority was assigned to the AJ 37 attack variant. The seventh Viggen became the prototype for the tandem two-seat SK 37 operational trainer performing its maiden flight on 2 July 1970. The first production AJ 37 followed on 23February 1971, and initial deliveries began to Flgflottilj 7 (F7) on 21 June 1971. Introduction of the SK 37 into the Linköping assembly plant at an early stage was to prove a vital factor in the successful service phase-in of the Viggen. Evolution of the fighter variant was viewed as a somewhat longer-term programme, so that adequately advanced intercept radar and suitable air-air weapons could be developed to endow the SwAF with the greatly improved air defence capabilities it sought. Whereas changes to the Viggen to produce the SK 37 trainer and the SF 37/SH 37 reconnaissance variants were minimal and confined mostly to areas dictated by mission requirements, those foreseen for the JA 37 fighter were more fundamental, so much so it was soon being viewed as a second-generation aircraft.

In Service

Re-equipment of three wings operational on the AJ 37s began in mid-1971 and the first squadron of F7 Wing at Såtenäs was declared operational early in 1973. Conversion of F15 at Söderhamn and F6 at Karlsborg was initiated in 1974. SF 37s and SH 37s entered service with F13 at Norrköping, F17 at Ronneby and F21 at Luleå, while all Viggen Wings operated SK 37 trainers. First deliveries of JA 37 fighters were made to F13 at Norrköping in 1979 replacing J35F Drakens, and continued with F1 at Ronneby and F21 at Luleå.

The service life of the Viggen with the SwAF can be summarised as follows. F4 at Frösön was formed on two units of JA 37s, Division 1 (David Röd) and Division 2 (David Blå) between 1983 and 2003; for a short period between 1999 and 2003 it also operated a unit of SK 37s and SK 37Es. F6 at Karlsborg operated two Divisions of AJ 37s (1: Filip Röd; 2 Filip Blå) between 1987 and 1993 together with the closure of its base. F7 at Såtenäs was made up of three units of AJ 37s starting in 1973: Division 1 (Gustav Röd), Division 2 (Gustav Blå) and Division 3 (Gustav Gul). Up to 1974 F7 also operated a unit of SK 37s while Division 3 was disbanded in 1977; the other two units became the first to convert to the Gripen between 1997 and 1998.

F10 at Ängelholm had only one Division (Johan Röd) and flew AJ 37s, SF 37s and SH 37s from July 1993 to April 2000 when it also converted onto the Gripen. F13 at Norrköping flew a unit (Division 1 Martin Röd) of SF 37s from 1976 and additionally SH 37s as from the following year; Division 2 (Martin Blå) continued to fly Drakens until the arrival of the JA 37 in 1982. Both Divisions closed down in summer 1993. F15 at Söderhamn began by operating a unit of SK 37s towards the end of 1974 until it formed two Divisions of JA 37s, Olle Röd in 1975 and Olle Blå the following year, continuing to fly the type up disbandment in June 1997. F16 at Uppsala was equipped with two Divisions of JA 37s (Petter Blå and Petter Gul) between 1986 and 2003. F17 at Ronneby was formed Division 1 (Quintus Röd) on SF/SH 37s in 1978 while Division Two (Quintus Blå) converted from Drakens to JA 37s in 1982. Division 1 reverted to the air defence role in summer of 1993 and received JA 37s until both units converted to the Gripen towards the end of 2002.

F21 at Luleå was to become the unit to hold onto the Viggen for the longest period of operational life. Division 1 (Urban Röd) was formed on the SF/SH 37 in July 1979 while Division 2 (Urban Blå) and Division 3 (Urban Gul) began to operate JA 37s in July 1983. In 2003 Division 1 was expanded to include new deliveries of the SK 37E thus becoming a multi-role unit until final retirement of the Viggen was marked at Luleå with a ceremony on 25 November 2005.

Viggen Described

As already mentioned, the most prominent feature of the Viggen's configuration is its large canard delta wing. The main wing had two-section hydraulic-actuated powered elevons on each trailing edge, which could be operated differentially or in unison. It had compound sweep on the leading edge, with the outer sections of the wing having an extended leading-edge. The canard foreplane had trailing edge flaps. Extensive use was made of metal-bonded honeycomb panels for wing, control surfaces, foreplane flaps, rudder, main landing gear doors and other areas.

The fuselage was of conventional all-metal semi-monocoque structure, using light metal forgings and heat-resistant plastic bonding. Titanium was used for the engine firewall and some other areas. Four plate-type airbrakes were fitted, one on each side and two below the fuselage. The nose cone could be pulled forward on tracks for easy radar access. The main fin had a powered rudder and could be folded down to port to permit passage through low hangar doors. The retractable tricycle under- carriage was designed for a maximum rate of sink of 985 ft/min. The twin-wheel nose unit was power steerable and retracted forward. Each main unit had two wheels in tandem and retracted inward into the main wing and fuselage as the main oleos shortened during retraction.

Powerplant of all variants – except the JA 37 – was the Volvo Flygmotot RM8A (a supersonic development of Pratt & Whitney's JT8D-22) turbofan, fitted with a Swedish-developed afterburner and thrust reverser. It was rated at 14,770lbst dry and 26,015lb st in afterburner. The JA 37 had the more powerful RM8B ver-sion, rated at 16,203bst dry and 28,108lbst in afterburner. An interesting feature of the thrust reversers was that the doors were actuated automatically by the compression of the oleo as the nose gear struck the runway, thrust being deflected for ward via three annular slots in the ejector wall. Fuel was contained in one tank in each wing, a saddle tank over the engine, one tank in each side of the fuselage and one behind the cockpit. The central fuselage tank was kept continuously filled from the other tanks. An external tank could be carried on the centreline pylon was normally a permanent fit on the two-seat SK37 as this variant lacked the forward fuselage tank.

The fully adjustable rocket-assisted ejection seat was made by Saab-Scania. Cockpit pressurisation, heating and air-conditioning was achieved by engine bleed air. The clamshell canopy hinged rearward and the windscreen could withstand a 2.2lb bird impact at 683 mph. The JA 37 cockpit was redesigned and optimised for the intercept mission. The SK 37 had individual canopies and twin periscopes were fitted between front and rear canopies.

A pair of JA37 Viggens finished in low-viz grey colours. In the foreground is 37350 (13-40). In 1982 two aircraft from F13 were finished in trial camouflage of different overall grey tones. Note the formidable 30mm ventral cannon (left) (SAAB-Scania)

The two-seat Viggen version, the SK 37, retains all the multi-purpose combat capabilities of its single-seat stablemate. Note the periscope fairings between the two cockpits. 15-63 is 27807 that became a SK 37E in 1999 and was sent to the scrapyard in 2006 (SAAB-Scania)

handled by a Saa-bScania CK-37 digital computer. Both SF 37 and SH 37 reconnaissance versions could carry two AAMs on the outboard wing stations for self-defence. Other external mission equipment included drop-tanks under the fuselage and ECM pods on each of the inboard underwing pylons. The SH 37 could carry a drop-tank on the centreline hardpoint, a night recce pod on the port hardpoint and a long-range camera pod or Red Baron night recce pod to starboard. The JA 37 permanently carried a ventral pack, offset to port of the centreline, containing one 30mm Oerlikon KCA long-ranae cannon with 150 rounds, firing at the rate of 1,350 rounds per minute. This gun installation permitted retention of the three under-fuselage hardpoints. This version of the Viggen also had an improved fire control system and an advanced tar get search and acquisition system. Other armament could include two RB71 (BAe Dynamics Skyflash) and four RM24 (Sidewinder) AAMS. Four pods containing a total of twenty-four 135mm rockets could be carried for the attack role.

Versions
Total production of the initial AJ 37 was of 106 examples (37001-37108) and represented the all-weather attack version that began to replace the Saab A32A Lansen in SwAF service in mid-1971. It also had a secondary interceptor capability; some of these Viggens were upgraded and redesignated AJS 37. Eighteen examples of the SK 37 two-seat trainer were built (37800-37817), some of which were upgraded to SK 37Es. The SF 37, of which 28 examples were built (37950-37977) was a single-seat all-weather armed photo-reconnaissance fighter intended to replace the S35E Draken. First flight of the first SF37 took place on 21 May 1973 and apart from four cameras in the nose it could also carry an external ventral pod with additional photographic equipment. Some were upgraded and became AJSF 37s . Ordered at the same time as the SF 37, the SH 37 was principally a radar-reconnaissance fighter of which 28 examples were produced (37900-27927); its upgrade was known as the AJSH 37.

The lion's share of Viggen production went to the JA 37 all-weather air-defence fighter of which 149 were built (37301-37449). Four AJ 37s were used in the development of the new fighter with the first being earmarked for control systems tests, flying for the first time on 4 June 1974 while the fourth modified AJ 37 flew in May 1975 and was assigned for electronics testing and later weapon system development. The fifth aircraft in the batch was built as a JA 37 from the outset and performed its maiden flight on 15 December 1975. A series of avionic and software upgrades were made on several JA 37s that were eventually redesignated JA 37C, JA 37D and JA 37Di.

A final mention must be made of the Saab 37X, intended as an export version that was essentially similar to the JA 37. Notwithstanding an aggressive export campaign no foreign sales of the Viggen were ever achieved. However three courses lasting six months each were organised for Austrian Air Force (AAF) pilots under 'Project Polar Light' by F21 at Luleå. This training enabled Austrian pilots to gain experience in flying advanced weapon systems and they flew the type under operational conditions in Sweden.

There were two independent hydraulic systems, each with an engine driven pump and an auxiliary electrically operated stand-by pump for emergency use. About 50 electronic units, weighing about 1,323lb, went into the Viggen. Flight equipmentation included and automatic speed control, HUD (Smiths in JA 37, Marconi-Elliott in other variants), AGA aircraft attitude instruments and radio, Phillips air data computer in 37 and Garret-Air Research in JA 37, Honeywell radar altimeter, Decca Doppler Type 72 navigation equipment and L.M. Ericson radar. There was a SATT radar warning system, Svenska Radio radar display system and ECM and AIL Tactical lnstrument Landing System. Most electronic equipment was connected to the central digital computer that could check out and monitor these systems on the ground or in flight. The JA 37 had a ram air intake beneath the fuselage for electronics cooling.

All armament on the Viggen was carried externally, on seven permanent attachment points, three under the fuselage and two under each wing. An additional hardpoint could be fitted under each wing if necessary. Primary armament consisted of the Saab RB04E or RB05A air-to-surface missiles (ASMS) for the attack role and pods of Bofors 135mm air-to-surface rockets, bombs or podded 30mm Aden guns. TheAJ 37 could be adapted for the intercept role armed with RB24 (Sidewinder) or RB28 (Falcon) AAMS. Fire control was

Colour Art All Colour Art © Richard J. Caruana – 2020

Serial: *37-1*

Fate:
*Scrapped by the
Flygvapenmuseum, in 2012*

Saab 37 Viggen, *37-1, first of eight prototypes (37-1 to 37-8) shown in its final form. It performed its maiden flight on 8 February 1967 piloted by Erik Dahlström. Natural metal overall with black radome and lettering. National markings in six positions. Note marking below front canard*

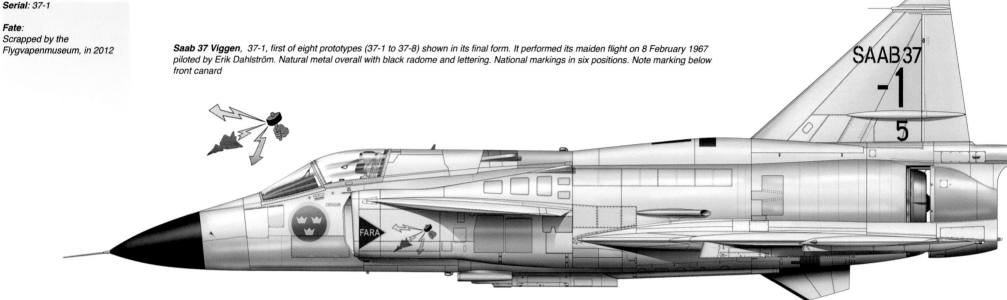

Serial: *37058*

Struck off Charge:
01.10.82
Other Identities:
6-58

Fate:
*Preserved at the Västerås
Flygmuseum, Stockholm-
Västerås Airport*

Saab 37 Viggen, *37-6, 56-752, sixth of eight prototypes (37-1 to 37-8); as displayed at the Paris Air Show, Le Bourget, 1969. Natural metal overall with black radome and lettering. National markings in six positions. Saab logo on nose in black with blue and yellow arrowheads*

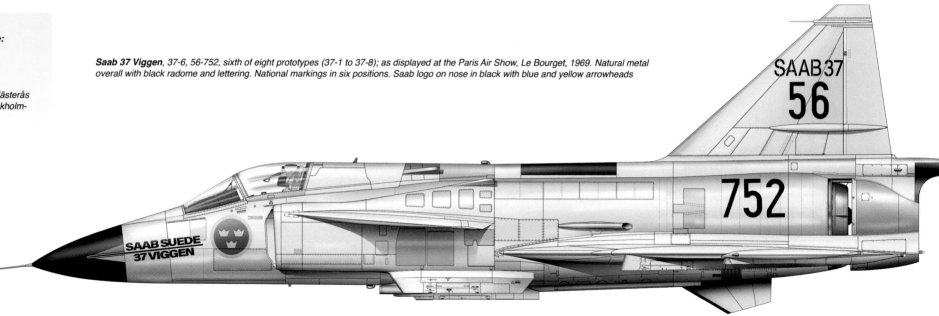

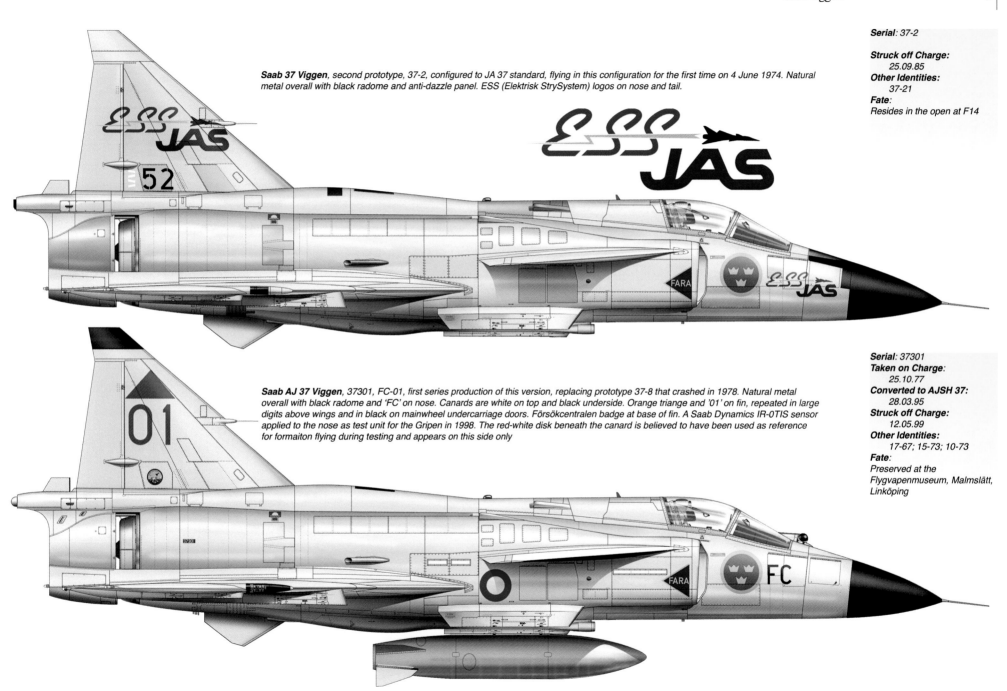

Saab 37 Viggen, second prototype, 37-2, configured to JA 37 standard, flying in this configuration for the first time on 4 June 1974. Natural metal overall with black radome and anti-dazzle panel. ESS (Elektrisk StrySystem) logos on nose and tail.

Serial: 37-2

Struck off Charge:
25.09.85
Other Identities:
37-21
Fate:
Resides in the open at F14

Saab AJ 37 Viggen, 37301, FC-01, first series production of this version, replacing prototype 37-8 that crashed in 1978. Natural metal overall with black radome and 'FC' on nose. Canards are white on top and black underside. Orange triange and '01' on fin, repeated in large digits above wings and in black on mainwheel undercarriage doors. Försökcentralen badge at base of fin. A Saab Dynamics IR-0TIS sensor applied to the nose as test unit for the Gripen in 1998. The red-white disk beneath the canard is believed to have been used as reference for formaiton flying during testing and appears on this side only

Serial: 37301
Taken on Charge:
25.10.77
Converted to AJSH 37:
28.03.95
Struck off Charge:
12.05.99
Other Identities:
17-67; 15-73; 10-73
Fate:
Preserved at the
Flygvapenmuseum, Malmslätt,
Linköping

Serial: *37022*
Taken on Charge:
20.03.73
Struck off Charge:
30.06.94
Other Identities:
6-22
Fate:
Scrapped at Stena Metall

Saab AJ 37 Viggen, *37022, 7-22, Flygflottilji F7, September 1973. Natural metal overall with all numbers in black. Standard national markings. Zapped with Luftwaffe JBG 33 markings on the fin (red on port and blue on starboard) and JBG36 on rear fuselage (both sides). Note early type ventral fin*

Serial: *37053*
Taken on Charge:
06.06.74
Converted to AJS 37:
06.12.94
Struck off Charge:
23.06.97
Other Identities:
15-13; 10-13
Fate:
Scrapped

Saab AJ 37 Viggen, *37053, Flygflottilji F7, Såtenäs, as displayed at the Farnborough Air Show of 1974. Splinter camouflage of 093M Black Green; 326M Dark Green; 322M Medium Green and 507M Tan upper surfaces with 058M Blue Grey underside. Yellow codes and serial. Standard national markings in all positions. '53' repeated in black on mainwheel undercarriage doors*

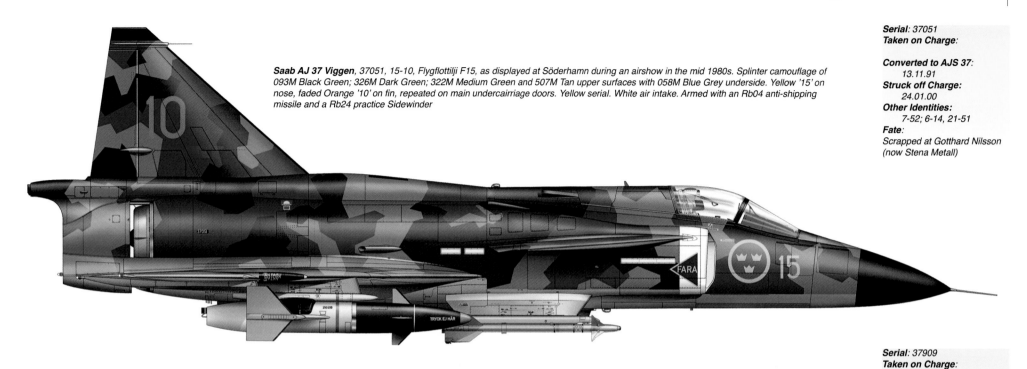

Saab AJ 37 Viggen, 37051, 15-10, Flygflottilji F15, as displayed at Söderhamn during an airshow in the mid 1980s. Splinter camouflage of 093M Black Green; 326M Dark Green; 322M Medium Green and 507M Tan upper surfaces with 058M Blue Grey underside. Yellow '15' on nose, faded Orange '10' on fin, repeated on main undercairriage doors. Yellow serial. White air intake. Armed with an Rb04 anti-shipping missile and a Rb24 practice Sidewinder

Serial: 37051
Taken on Charge:

Converted to AJS 37:
 13.11.91
Struck off Charge:
 24.01.00
Other Identities:
 7-52; 6-14, 21-51
Fate:
Scrapped at Gotthard Nilsson
(now Stena Metall)

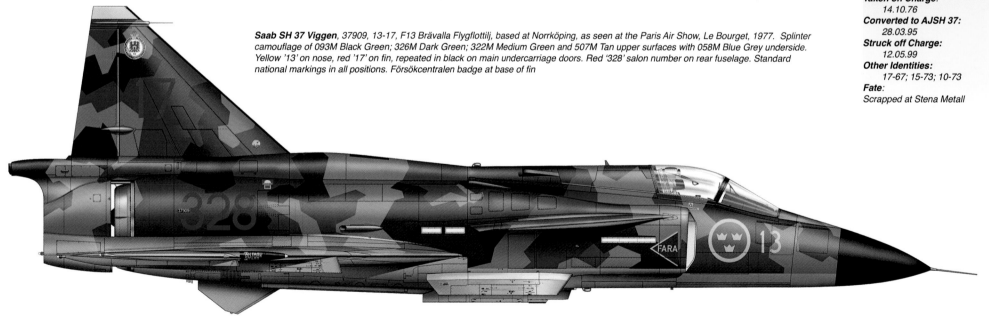

Saab SH 37 Viggen, 37909, 13-17, F13 Brävalla Flygflottilj, based at Norrköping, as seen at the Paris Air Show, Le Bourget, 1977. Splinter camouflage of 093M Black Green; 326M Dark Green; 322M Medium Green and 507M Tan upper surfaces with 058M Blue Grey underside. Yellow '13' on nose, red '17' on fin, repeated in black on main undercarriage doors. Red '328' salon number on rear fuselage. Standard national markings in all positions. Försökcentralen badge at base of fin

Serial: 37909
Taken on Charge:
 14.10.76
Converted to AJSH 37:
 28.03.95
Struck off Charge:
 12.05.99
Other Identities:
 17-67; 15-73; 10-73
Fate:
Scrapped at Stena Metall

Serial: *37035*
Taken on Charge:
04.02.74
Converted to AJS 37:
07.08.92
Struck off Charge:
12.05.99
Other Identities:
7-35; 7-35 again after 6-35
Fate:
Scrapped at Säve

Saab AJ 37 Viggen, *37035; 6-35; Flygflottilji F6; Karlsborg; 1990. Splinter camouflage of 093M Black Green; 326M Dark Green; 322M Medium Green and 507M Tan upper surfaces with 058M Blue Grey underside. Yellow '6' on nose; Orange '35' on fin, repeated in black on main undercarriage doors. Standard national markings*

Serial: *37058*
Taken on Charge:
25.07.74
Converted to AJS 37:
18.05.92
Struck off Charge:
01.10.99
Other Identities:
6-58
Fate:
Front fuselage preserved at the Volvo Museum at Arendal on Hisingen, Gothenburg .

Saab AJ 37 Viggen, *37058, 7-58, Flygflottilji F7, Satenäs, 1975. Splinter camouflage of 093M Black Green; 326M Dark Green; 322M Medium Green and 507M Tan upper surfaces with 058M Blue Grey underside. '7' on nose in yellow, 58 in red on fin, repeated in black on main undercarriage doors*

Saab AJS 37 Viggen, 37081, 15-26, Flygflottilji F15, Söderhamn, 1993. Splinter camouflage of 093M Black Green; 326M Dark Green; 322M Medium Green and 507M Tan upper surfaces with 058M Blue Grey underside. Yellow '15' on nose, Fading Orange '61' on fin, repeated in black on mainwheel undercarriage doors. Standard national markings in all positions. Serial in yellow

Serial: 37081
Taken on Charge: 18.08.75
Converted to AJS 37: 15.12.92
Struck off Charge: 08.09.00
Other Identities: 7-76; 10-76
Fate: Front fuselage section preserved at F15 Museum, Söderhamn

Saab AJ 37 Viggen, 37094, 10-57, Flygflottilji F10, 1996. Weathered splinter camouflage of 093M Black Green; 326M Dark Green; 322M Medium Green and 507M Tan upper surfaces with 058M Blue Grey underside. Faded Orange '57' on fin, repeated in black on mainwheel undercarriage doors. '10' in yellow on nose. Unit badge on fin and what appears to be a No 41 Squadron (RAF) zap also on fin. Standard national markings in all positions

Serial: 37094
Taken on Charge: 14.10.76
Struck off Charge: 12.05.99
Other Identities: 6-05; 21-57
Fate: Preserved at the Aeromuseum, Säve Airport, Gothenburg

Serial: *37083*
Taken on Charge:
    18.08.75
Struck off Charge:
    02.12.96
Other Identities:
    15-28; 6-28;7-05
Fate:
Front fuselage preserved at the F15 Flygmuseum, Söderhamn

Saab AJS 37 Viggen, *37083, 10-07, Flygflottilji F10, Ängelhom, 1995. Splinter camouflage of 093M Black Green; 326M Dark Green; 322M Medium Green and 507M Tan upper surfaces with 058M Blue Grey underside. Red vertical tail surfaces with Christmas motif (signed 'Preben') and unit badge. Codes on nose and tail in yellow with '07' repeated in black on mainwheel undercarriage doors. Standard national markings in all positions.*

Saab AJS 37 Viggen, *37076, 10-76, Flygflottilji F10 (1st Squadron), Ängelholm, 2000. Splinter camouflage of 093M Black Green; 326M Dark Green; 322M Medium Green and 507M Tan upper surfaces with 058M Blue Grey underside. Yellow '10' on nose, red '76' on fin over what appears a repaint to cover a previous identity (15-21), repeated in black on the mainwheel door covers, and in large white numerals above the wings. Serial in yellow on fuselage with last three digits repeated above the rudder. Standard national markings in all positions*

Serial: *37076*
Taken on Charge:
    14.04.75
Modified to AJS 37:
    29.04.94
Struck off Charge:
    12.05.99
Other Identities:
    15-29
Fate:
Scrapped

Serial: 37027
Taken on Charge:
    02.08.73
Converted to AJS 37:
    28.09.93
Struck off Charge:
    10.06.01
Other Identities:
    7-57; FC-27; 6-27
Fate:
Preserved at the Teknikens och
sjöfartens hus, Malmö

Saab AJS 37 Viggen, 37027, 10-57, Flygflottilji F10, (1st Squadron), to mark disbandment April 2000. Red overall with yellow '57' on tail and white lettering 'The Show Must Go On'. White ghost motif on fin, repeated on nose with the lettering of the fuselage repeated in yellow within a white disk, all outline in black. The white 'ghost' was repeated on the top and bottom of both wings

Serial: *37333*
Taken on Charge:
18.11.82
Struck off Charge:
25.10.00
Other Identities:
4-33
Fate:
Scrapped by Gotthard Nilsson (now Stena Metall)

Saab JA 37 Viggen, *37333, 17-33, Flygflottilji F17, Ronneby, 1982. Natural metal overall but with a nose from a splinter camouflaged aircraft (093M Black Green, 326M Dark Green, 322M Medium Green and 507M Tan upper surfaces with 058M Blue Grey underside); Orange '33' on fin with '17' in yellow on nose. Standard national markings in all positions*

Serial: *37330*
Taken on Charge:
27.08.82
Other Identities:
16-30

Saab JA 37 Viggen, *37330, 13-30, Flygflottilji F13, Norrköping, 1988. Splinter camouflage of 093M Black Green; 326M Dark Green; 322M Medium Green and 507M Tan upper surfaces with 058M Blue Grey underside. Orange '30' on fin repeated on mainwheel undercarriage doors, yellow '13' on nose and serial on rear fuselage. Unit badge on fin. Standard national markings in all positions*

Serial: *37350*
Taken on Charge:
08.10.82
Struck off Charge:
28.11.00
Other Identities:
4-40; 17-50
Fate:
Scrapped by Gotthard Nilsson (now Stena Metall)

Saab JA 37 Viggen, *37350, 13-40, Flygflottilji F13, Norrköping,1982. One of the two JA 37s experimentally finished in Mörkgrå 033 (FS36251) overall. '13' on nose and '40' on fin in black; the latter repeated on mainwheel undercarriage doors. Unit badge on fin. Also introduced the reduced size national markings in all positions; 525mm diameter on nose; 710mm diamater on wings*

Serial: *37329*
Taken on Charge:
21.09.82
Converted to JA 37Di:
09.11.01
Other Identities:
4-29
Fate:
Scrapped by Stena Metall

Saab JA 37 Viggen, *37329, 13-69, Flygflottilji F13; Norrköping, 1982. All lettereing in black except for serial which is yellow. Unit badge on fin. Reduced size national markings in all positions*

Serial: *37411*
Taken on Charge:
26.05.86
Other Identities:
21-31
Fate:
Scrapped

Saab JA 37 Viggen, 37411, 16-11, Flygflottilji F16, In official colours of the official Flygvapnet Viggen display aircraft, June 2000. Mörkgrå 033 (FS.36251) with dark grey bands over the upper surfaces and Grå 032 (FS.36463) undersides. Orange triangle and '11' on fin, the latter repeated in black on mainwheel undercarriage doors. '16' on nose in black, serial in yellow. Dark grey badge of 3.FU-komp/F16 badge on rear fuselage, repeated below the wings. Badge of 3.div/F16 in light grey just ahead of fuselage airbrakes. Reduced size national markings on nose and above wings, black only below the wings

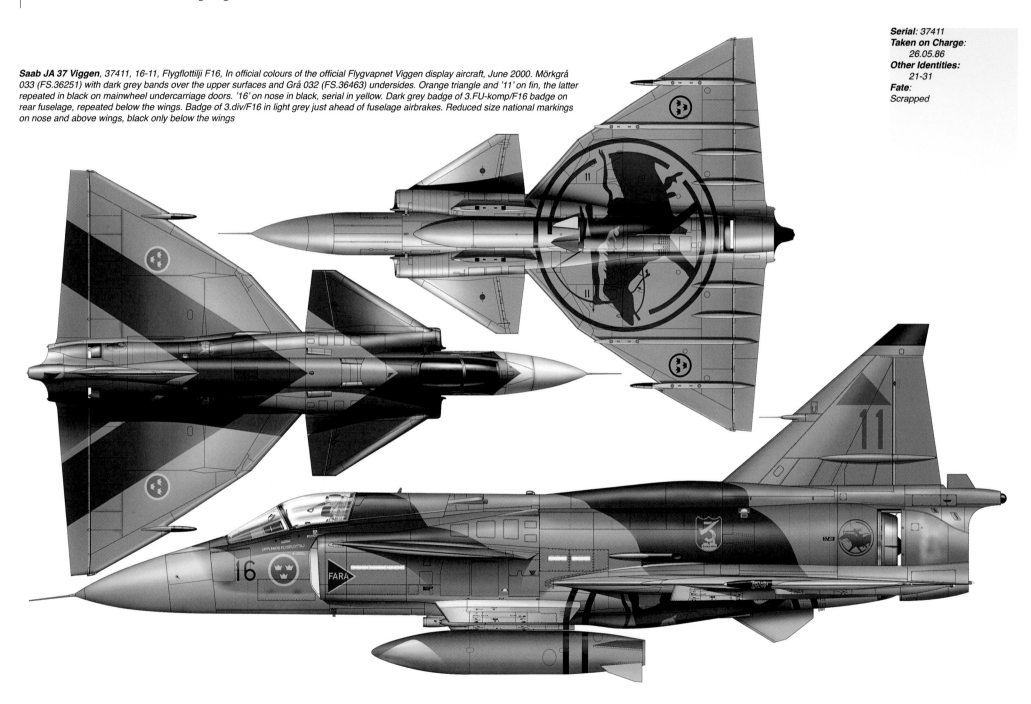

Saab JA 37 Viggen, 37394, 17-47, Flygflottilji F17, Ronebby, 2002. Mörkgrå 033 (FS.36251) and Grå 032 (FS.36463) finish. Yellow/blue trim to leading edges of all flying surfaces. Orange triangle and '47' on fin, the latter repeated in high letters above the wings ('4' port, '7' starboard). Black lettering on base of fin indicates the period that the unit operated the Viggen before transitioning onto the Gripen in 2002. Reduced side national markings in all positions. Serial in yellow on rear fuselage, unit badge on fin, 1st Division badge aft of cockpit

Serial: 37394
Taken on Charge:
  19.02.85
Struck off Charge:
  24.03.03
Other Identities:
  4-64
Fate:
Scrapped by Stena Metall

Serial: *37439*
Taken on Charge:
   13.03.89
Struck off Charge:
   18.01.01
Other Identities:
   16.39
Fate:
*Scrapped by Gotthard Nilsson
(now Stena Metall)*

Saab JA 37 Viggen, *37439, 4-01, Flygflottilji F4, Östersund-Frösön, 1989. Mörkgrå 033 (FS.36251) and Grå 032 (FS.36463) finish. Codes and triangle on fin in Orange, with '01' repeated in large numbers above the wings, '0' above port, '1' above starboard. Reduced size national markings in all positions. '01' in black on mainwheel undercarriage doors. Unit markings on fin*

Serial: *37412*
Taken on Charge:
   19.09.86
Converted to JA 37Di:
   26.06.98
Other Identities:
   21-32; 17-12; 4-12
Fate:
*Preserved at Teknikland,
Östersund*

Saab JA 37 Viggen, *37412, 13-32, Flygflottilji F13,as seen at RAF Coningsby (UK), 1989. Mörkgrå 033 (FS.361251) and Grå 032 (FS.36463). Black codes on nose and fin; (serial painted over). '32' repeated in black on mainwheel undercarriage doors. Unit badge on fin. 2.div/F13 'Martin Blå' crest in dark grey on port side fuselage only. Reduced size national markings in all positions*

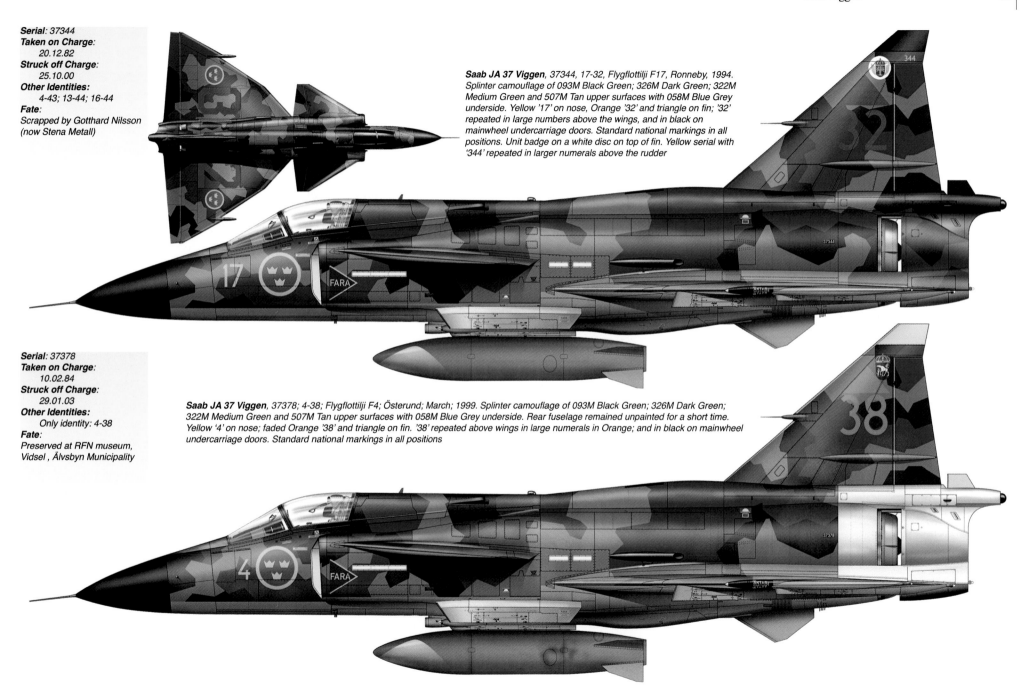

Serial: 37344
Taken on Charge:
20.12.82
Struck off Charge:
25.10.00
Other Identities:
4-43; 13-44; 16-44
Fate:
Scrapped by Gotthard Nilsson
(now Stena Metall)

Saab JA 37 Viggen, 37344, 17-32, Flygflottilji F17, Ronneby, 1994. Splinter camouflage of 093M Black Green; 326M Dark Green; 322M Medium Green and 507M Tan upper surfaces with 058M Blue Grey underside. Yellow '17' on nose, Orange '32' and triangle on fin; '32' repeated in large numbers above the wings, and in black on mainwheel undercarriage doors. Standard national markings in all positions. Unit badge on a white disc on top of fin. Yellow serial with '344' repeated in larger numerals above the rudder

Serial: 37378
Taken on Charge:
10.02.84
Struck off Charge:
29.01.03
Other Identities:
Only identity: 4-38
Fate:
Preserved at RFN museum,
Vidsel , Älvsbyn Municipality

Saab JA 37 Viggen, 37378; 4-38; Flygflottilji F4; Österund; March; 1999. Splinter camouflage of 093M Black Green; 326M Dark Green; 322M Medium Green and 507M Tan upper surfaces with 058M Blue Grey underside. Rear fuselage remained unpainted for a short time. Yellow '4' on nose; faded Orange '38' and triangle on fin. '38' repeated above wings in large numerals in Orange; and in black on mainwheel undercarriage doors. Standard national markings in all positions

Serial: 37410
Taken on Charge:
  24.04.86
Struck off Charge:
  27.03.03
Other Identities:
  21-30
Fate:
Preserved at Österlen's
Aviation Museum, Gärsnäs ,
Simrishamn Municipality

Saab JA 37 Viggen, 37410, 16-10, Flygflottilji F16 (3rd Squadron), Uppsala, 2003. Mörkgrå 033 (FS.36251) and Grå 032 (FS.36463) finish with red tail with black Indian on Horse motif on vertical tail surfaces. Yellow serial on rear fuselage with 'P10' in red on top of fin. '16' on nose in black, '10' also in black on mainwheel undercarriage doors. Reduced size national markings, 525mm diameter on fuselage, 710mm diameter on wings. 3rd Squadron badge aft of cockpit. Special scheme for the retirement of the type

Saab JA 37 Viggen, 37432, 16-32 'Blå Petter', Flygflottilji F16, Uppsala, 2001. Blue overall with yellow trim to wing and foreplane leading edges, and cross on vertical tail surfaces. '16' on nose in yellow. P32 on fin in black over grey tip. The markings on the rear fuselage are repeated above the wings, port on starboard and vice versa. Special scheme to commemorate the 75th Anniversary of the Swedish Air Force

Serial: *37432*
Taken on Charge:
16.06.88
Struck off Charge:
25.01.02
Other Identities:
Only identity: 16-32
Fate:
Preserved at Gotland's Defense Museum, Tingstäde

Serial: 37304
Taken on Charge:
 26.10.79
Struck off Charge:
 15.03.01
Other Identities:
 13-44; 17-04; 21-04

Saab JA 37 Viggen, 37304, 21-01, Flygflottilji F21 Ronneby-Kallinge, 2000. Splinter camouflage of 093M Black Green; 326M Dark Green; 322M Medium Green and 507M Tan upper surfaces with 058M Blue Grey underside. Purple vertical tail surfaces with Hagar cartoon on both sides. Codes and serial in yellow; '01' repeated in black on mainwheel undercarriage doors and in large numerals in Orange above wings. Standard national markings in all positions. Commemorative scheme when the unit converted onto the Gripen

Serial: *37347*
Taken on Charge:
  19.02.82
Struck off Charge:
  05.09.88
Restored & Converted to Ja37Di:
  14.04.98
Other Identities:
  13-37;16-37
Fate:
*Preserved at HM Hadtörténeti Intézet
és Múzeum, Hungary*

Saab JA 37Di Viggen, *37347, 16-47, operated by the Försökscenttralen as a prototype for the Mod D Interoperability upgrade. Mörkgrå 033 (FS.36251) and Grå 032 (FS.36463) Blue vertical tail suraces with yellow cross which has a black drop shadow; lettering on fin in black (on port side only). '16' on nose in black painted over, triangle and '47 on starboard side in Orange, repeated in black on top of fin and on mainwheel undercarriage legs. Black/white calibration marks on starboard side only. Orange band around nose. Reduced size national markings in all positions. Note that originally it carried '47' in large Orange numbers above the wings but these were later deleted*

Serial: *37326*
Taken on Charge:
  19.04.82
Converted to JA 37Di:
  14.01.02
Other Identities:
  13-26
Fate:
Preserved at Svedinos Bil-och Flygmuseum, Ugglarp

Saab JA 37Di Viggen, *37326, 17-26; Flygflottilji F17 (1 JaktSquadronen) Satenäs , now preserved at the Svedinos Bil-och Flygmuseum. Splinter camouflage of 093M Black Green, 326M Dark Green, 322M Medium Green and 507M Tan upper surfaces with 058M Blue Grey underside. Orange code and triangle on fin (repeated in big numbers over the wings), yellow '17' on nose. Serial in yellow with '326' repeated above the rudder. Unit badge on fin, 1st Squadron badge aft of cockpit. Standard national markings in all positions*

Serial: *37386*
Taken on Charge:
  11.09.84
Modified to JA 37Di:
  09.06.98
Other Identities:
  4-56; 17-46
Fate:
Front fuselage section preserved at Svedinos Bil- och Flygmuseum, Ugglarp

Saab JA 37Di Viggen, *37386, 4-46; Flygflottilji F4; Österund-Frösön, September-December 2004. Mörkgrå 033 (FS.36152) and Grå 032 (FS.36373) scheme. National markings in medium grey on wings with large numerals 46 in Orange above wings. Storsjö 'Great Lake Monster' on nose and Jämtland region colours and crest on fin; 2 Division of F4 badge on a white disc aft of cockpit*

Serial: *37402*
Taken on Charge:
16.06.88
Modified to JA 37Di:
10.12.98
Other Identities:
17-02

Saab JA 37Di Viggen, *37402, 21-02, Flygflottilji F21 (1st Squadron), Luleå, 2004. Mörkgrå 033 (FS.36251) and Grå 032 (FS.36463)finish with yellow and blue 'sun' tail with black trim. Yellow serial on rear fuselage. Black '21' on nose and Orange '21' on fin, the latter repeated in large numerals above the wings; '0' above port and '2' above starboard. '02' in black on mainwheel undercarriage doors. Reduced size national markings in all positions. 1st Squadron badge aft of cockpit*

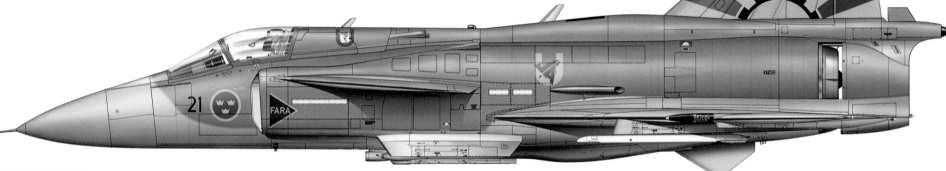

Serial: *37350*
Taken on Charge:
08.10.82
Struck off Charge:
28.11.00
Other Identities:
13-40; 4-40
Fate:
Scrapped by Gotthard Nilsson (now Stena Metall)

Saab JA 37Di Viggen, *37350, 17-50; Flygflottilji F17 (1st Squadron), Satenäs. One of the two experimentally finished in Mörkgrå 033 FS36251 overall when coded 13-40, and which remained in this finish for the rest of its service life, shown in a highly weathered finish. '17' on nose in black, code 50 and triangle on fin in Orange, '50' repeated in large numbers above the wings. Serial in yellow, last three digits repeated above rudder. Unit badge on fin, 1st Squadron badge aft of cockpit. Standard reduced size national markings in all positions*

Serial: *37445*
Taken on Charge:

Converted to JA 37D:
21-01-98
Other Identities:
16-45; 4-06
Fate:
Scrapped at Östersund

Saab JA 37D Viggen, *37445, 17-45, Flygflottilji F17, Exercise 'Baltic Link', August 2000. Mörkgrå 033 (FS.361251) and Grå 032 (FS.36463). Black '17' on nose. Orange triangle and '45' on fin, the latter repeatred above the wings in large numerals, and in black on mainwheel undercarriage legs. National markings of reduced size in all positions. Unit badge on fin. 2.div/F17, Quintus Blå badge aft of cockpit*

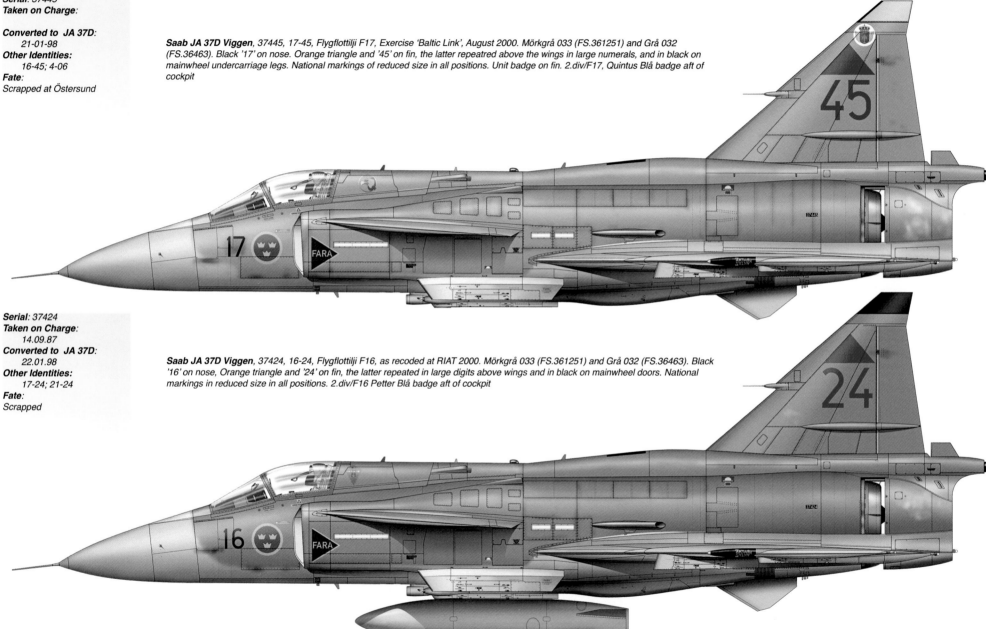

Serial: *37424*
Taken on Charge:
14.09.87
Converted to JA 37D:
22.01.98
Other Identities:
17-24; 21-24
Fate:
Scrapped

Saab JA 37D Viggen, *37424, 16-24, Flygflottilji F16, as recoded at RIAT 2000. Mörkgrå 033 (FS.361251) and Grå 032 (FS.36463). Black '16' on nose, Orange triangle and '24' on fin, the latter repeated in large digits above wings and in black on mainwheel doors. National markings in reduced size in all positions. 2.div/F16 Petter Blå badge aft of cockpit*

Saab JA 37Di Viggen, 37412, 4-12, Flygflottilji F4, Östersund-Frösön, November 2004. Gloss black overall with golden trim to top of fuselage and around the flying surfaces. Gold lettering. Reduced size national markings, also in gold, in all positions. 2.div/F4 'David Blå' badge aft of cockpit. Special colour scheme to mark the last meeting of the Viggen Order at F4's base

Serial: 37412
Taken on Charge:
 19.09.86
Converted to JA 37Di:
 26.06.98
Other Identities:
 21-32; 13-32; 17-12
Fate:
 Preserved at Teknikland,
 Östersund

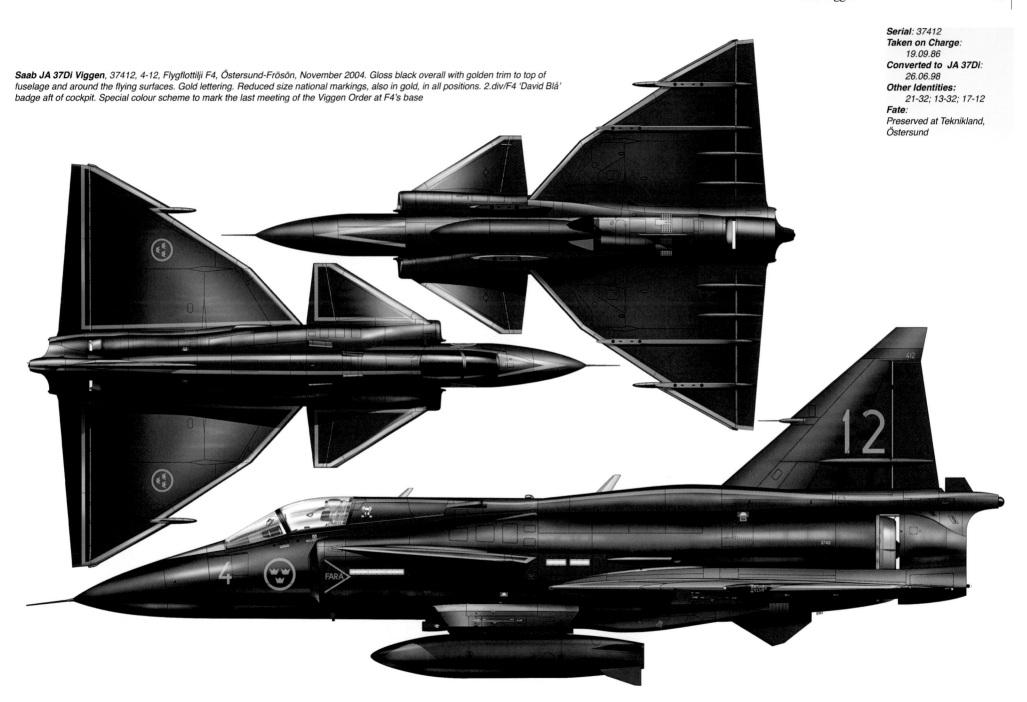

Serial: *37901*
Taken on Charge:
18.08.75
Modififed to AJSH 37:
14.11.95
Other Identities:
13-01; 21-51
Fate:
Preserved at the Nationaal Luchtvaart-Themapark Aviodrome, Lelystad, The Netherlands

Saab SH 37 Viggen, 37901, 10-01, Flygflottilji F10, Angelholm, 1993. Splinter camouflage of 093M Black Green; 326M Dark Green; 322M Medium Green and 507M Tan upper surfaces with 058M Blue Grey underside. Yellow '10' on nose, Orange '01' on fin repeated on mainwheel undercarriage doors. Unit badge on fin. Yellow serial on rear fuselage. Standard national markings in all positions

Serial: *37901*
Taken on Charge:
18.08.75
Modififed to AJSH 37:
14.11.95
Other Identities:
10-01; 21-51
Fate:
Preserved at the Nationaal Luchtvaart-Themapark Aviodrome, Lelystad, The Netherlands

Saab AJSH 37 Viggen, 37901, 13-01, Flygflottilji F13 (1st Squadron), Norrköping, 2002. Splinter camouflage of 093M Black Green; 326M Dark Green; 322M Medium Green and 507M Tan upper surfaces with 058M Blue Grey underside. Yellow '13' on nose, Orange '01' on fin. Serial in yellow, with '01' in black on mainwheel undercarriage doors. Unit badge on fin. Standard national markings on all positions. Note Rb04 anti-shipping missile carried under the wing

Serial: *37970*
Taken on Charge:
   27.06.79
Fate:
*Written off at Vingåker, collision
with 37969, 29.08.85*

Saab SF 37 Viggen, *37970, 13-20, Flygflottilji F13, Norrköping, 1982. Splinter camouflage of 093M Black Green; 326M Dark Green; 322M Medium Green and 507M Tan upper surfaces with 058M Blue Grey underside. Yellow '13' on nose, Orange '20' on fin, repeated in black on mainwheel undercarriage doors. Unit badge on fin. Standard national markings in all positions*

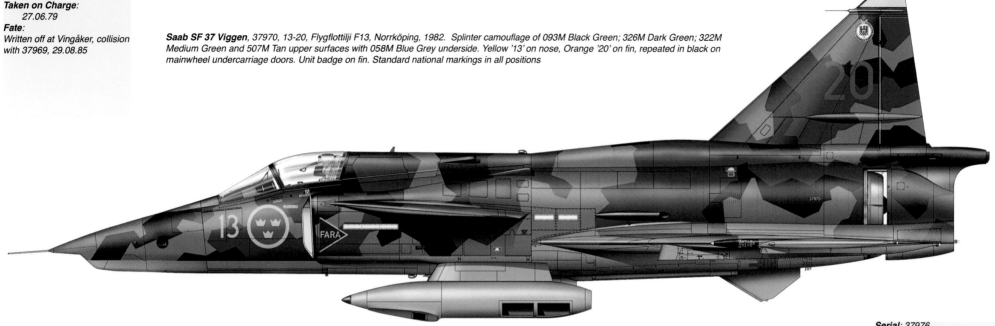

Saab SF 37 Viggen, *37976, 7-38, Flygflottilji F7, As recorded at RAF Fairford in 1995. Splinter camouflage of 093M Black Green; 326M Dark Green; 322M Medium Green and 507M Tan upper surfaces with 058M Blue Grey underside. '7' on nose in yellow, 38 in Orange on fin, repeated in black on mainwheel undercarriage doors. Yellow serial on rear fuselage with '976 repeated on top of fin. F21 Badge on fin. Standard national markings in all positions*

Serial: *37976*
Taken on Charge:
   01.02.80
Modififed to AJSF 37:
   12.05.97
Other Identities:
   21-66; 10-38; 21-66
Fate:
*Preserved at Ängelholm's
Aviation Museum*

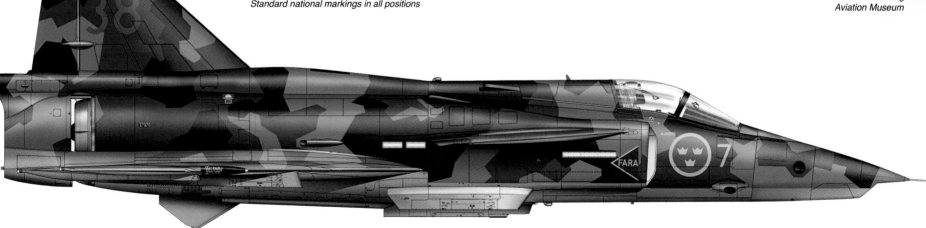

Saab SF 37 Viggen, 37950; 21-48; Flygflottilji F21 (1st Squadron) "Urban Röd"; Luleå; 2005. Flygflottilj; Mörkgrå 033 (FS.36152) upper surfaces with Grå 032 (FS.36373) undersides. Gradient tint on rear fuselage from light to dark blue at the rear with Wolf's head motif on vertical tail surfaces. Red ribbon with 'AKKTU-Stakkul' motto along fuselage. Red '48' on fin (repeated in black on mainwheel undercarrige doors), black '21' on nose. National markings in medium grey

Serial: 37950
Taken on Charge:
  11.01.79
Modififed to AJSF 37:
  11.02.97
Other Identities:
  Saab-95; 13-10; 10-10
Fate:
Preserved at Teknikland, Östersund
Note:
  Originally serialled 37033

Serial: *37965*
Taken on Charge:
    28.03.79
Modififed to AJSF 37:
    15.12.95
Struck off Charge
    08.02.99
Fate:
Scrapped at Stena Metal

Saab SF 37 Viggen, *37965, 21-54, Flygflottilji F21 (1st Squadron), Luleå-Kallax, 1987. Splinter camouflage of 093M Black Green; 326M Dark Green; 322M Medium Green and 507M Tan upper surfaces with 058M Blue Grey underside. Motif on nose in grey with red/white and black details. Orange '21' on nose and '54' on fin, the latter repeated on mainwheel undercarriage doors. Unit badge on fin. Serial in yellow with '965' repeated at top of fin. Standard national markings in all positions*

Serial: *37960*
Taken on Charge:
    27.04.79
Modififed to AJSF 37:
    12.09.96
Other Identities:
    21-60, 10-52
Fate:
Scrapped at Halmstad

Saab AJSF 37 Viggen, *37960, 21-52 but operated by Flygflottilji F10. Splinter camouflage of 093M Black Green; 326M Dark Green; 322M Medium Green and 507M Tan upper surfaces with 058M Blue Grey underside. Yellow '21' on nose with faded Orange '21' on fin, repeated in black on mainwheel undercarriage doors. Unit badge on fin. Serial in yellow with last three digits repeated above the rudder*

Serial: *37808*
Taken on Charge:
    03.01.74
Modififed to SK 37E:
    20.12.99
Other Identities:
    7-62; 7-11; 4-71; 21-71
Fate:
Preserved at the Musée de l'Air et de l'Espace, Le Bouget

Saab SK 37 Viggen, *37808, 15-62, Typinflygningsskolan 37 (TIS 37) after transfer from Flygflottilji F15 to F4, Östersund-Frösön, 1999. Splinter camouflage of 093M Black Green; 326M Dark Green; 322M Medium Green and 507M Tan upper surfaces with 058M Blue Grey underside. Yellow '15' on nose and serial on rear fuselage. Orange '62' (note faded '2') on fin, repeated in black on mainwheel undercarriage doors. F15 badge still carried on fin*

Serial: *37811*
Taken on Charge:
    06.06.75
Modififed to SK 37E:
    06.10.99
Other Identities:
    4-74, 21-73
Fate:
Preserved at the Musée Européen de l'Aviation de Chasse, Montélimar

Saab SK 37 Viggen, *37811, 15-58, Flygflottilji F15, Söderhamm, 1997. Flygflottilj; Mörkgrå 033 (FS.36251) and Grå 032 (FS.36463), the only two-seat Viggen to receive this finish. Black '15' on nose, Orange 58 and triangle on fin. Serial in yellow with '58' repeated in black on mainwheel undercarrige doors. Reduced size national markings in all positions*

Saab SK 37E Viggen, 37811, 21-73, Flygflottilji F21, Luleà. 2005. Flygflottilj; Mörkgrå 033 (FS.36251) and Grå 032 (FS.36463). Orange triangle and '73' on fin the latter repeated in black on mainwheel undercarrige doors; black '21' on nose. Red flash on fin. Standard reduced size national markings in all positions

Serial: *37811*
Taken on Charge:
06.06.75
Modififed to SK 37E:
06.10.99
Other Identities:
15-58;4-74
Fate:
Preserved at the Musée Européen de l'Aviation de Chasse, Montélimar

Saab SK 37E Viggen, 37813, FC-13, F21-73, Luleå, 2005. Weathered splinter camouflage of 093M Black Green; 326M Dark Green; 322M Medium Green and 507M Tan upper surfaces with 058M Blue Grey underside. Orange '13' on fin, repeated in black on mainwheel undercarriage doors. Orange band around nose. Yellow 'FC' on nose and serial on rear fuselage. Unit badge on fin. Orange band around nose indicating that together with 37809 (FC-48) was used by the Försökscentralen as flying test bed until retired in late 2007

Serial: *37813*
Taken on Charge:
11.05.76
Modififed to SK 37E:
07.11.00
Other Identities:
15-56; 4-75; 21-74
Struck off Charge:
27.06.07
Fate:
Offered to USA, gift failed; Scrapped at Stena Metall, 2007

Serial: *37447*
Taken on Charge:
06.04.90
Modififed to JA 37D:
28.08.98
Other Identities:
16-35
Fate:
Scrapped in Halmstad

Saab JA 37D Viggen, 37447, 21-35, Flygflottilji F21, as recoded at Beauvechain, Belgium, September 1999. Mörkgrå 033 (FS.361251) and Grå 032 (FS.36463). Black '21' on nose, orange triangle and '35' on fin, the latter repeated on mainwheel undercarriage doors. Note black nose tip. Unit badge on fin. Aircraft is armed with six Rb74 Sidewinder practice missiles

Serial: *37954*
Taken on Charge:
17.10.77
Modififed to AJSF 37:
18.10.96
Other Identities:
4-74, 21-73
Fate:
Preserved at the Lotnictwa Polskiego Museum, Krakow, Poland

Saab AJSF 37 Viggen, 37954; 21-54; Flygflottilji F21; Luleå-Kallax. Mörkgrå 033 (FS.36152) upper surfaces with Grå 032 (FS.36373) undersides. '54' repearted on mainwheel undercarriage doors. All lettering and national markings in dark grey as used during the final days of the Viggen's operations. '954' in small yellow numbers above fin. Note KB chaff/flare dispenser under the inner wing pylon